LUKE 4:18 KJV

The Spirit of the Lord is upon me, because he hath anointed me to preach the gospel to the poor; he hath sent me to heal the brokenhearted, to preach deliverance to the captives, and recovering of sight to the blind, to set at liberty them that are bruised.

FINDING YOUR VOICE

The Valley Experience

Compilation By:

Joyce M. H. Samuels

Revised by:

CBM Consultants

Copyright © 2016 by Joyce M. H. Samuels

Email: jmhsministries@gmail.com

Website: www.jmhsministries.com

All rights reserved. No part of this book may be reproduced in any form or by any electronic or mechanical means including information storage and retrieval systems, without permission in writing from the authors. The only exception is by a reviewer, who may quote short excerpts in a review.

Printed in the United States of America

First Printing, 2016

Revisions made by ©CBM Consultants
cbmconsult3@gmail.com

Scripture quotations, unless otherwise noted, are from the King James Version of the Bible.

While all stories in book are true, some names and identifying information in this book have been changed to protect the privacy of the individuals involved.

Special acknowledgement to Kelvin Tang for his outstanding work on the front and back cover.

Table of Content

Foreword

Acknowledgements

Deliverance from Destruction
Joyce M H. Samuels

Acknowledgements

My Walk with God
Kimberly A. DiStefano

Acknowledgements

Damaged Inside and Out
Serrica Jackson

Acknowledgements

God's Timing Not My Own
Evelyn M. Jackson

Acknowledgements

The Power of Deliverance
Valerie Johnson-Philson

Acknowledgements

My Name is Steven and I Found My Voice
Steven Layne

FOREWORD

    The reality is that we all face challenges in life. These challenges to us, in the midst of going through them, appear as if we may be punished for something we may have done. They create a feeling that God himself has forgotten about us and develop a silence that keeps us captured in our very own thoughts. The silence has a tendency to bring us into a valley experience where we wonder if we will ever arise from this low place and does God even hear us when we pray.

    It is in this place that the perseverance to be a better us emerges. It is in this place that the desire to be who God has called us to be is birthed from our valley experience. Our place of pain becomes our place of purposed birthed in the earth. We have become weakened from struggling with our own issues that we allow God's strength to be made perfect within us (II Corinthians 12:9). And out of the transition of power boasts the Voice from the Valley. The cry of help to the Father that surrenders your will for His. It is this expression that frees us from the prison of our past, the isolation of hurts, and the dungeon of disappointments.

Finding Your Voice in the Valley brings the blessing of knowing that your journey has worked out for your good (Romans 8:28). The glory now rest on your life that gives an identity to your being that cannot be duplicated or even taken from you, for you now know what it means to have been broken and mended. This experience carries with it a boldness that allows you to help others overcome by the word of your testimony and the blood of the Lamb (Revelation 12:11). And a holy indignation that states, I will never go back or be ashamed to share what God has done.

As you read this book, you have been given access to the lives of those that have found their voice in the valley. Though the experiences may differ the outcome is the same. VICTORY! They were once ensnared in a bondage that seemed unbreakable, but God! Be encouraged, be inspired and be stirred to find your voice in the valley and know that victory belongs to you.

Grace & Peace Apostles Lannice & Heather Collins

Acknowledgements

I would like to dedicate this chapter first to my Lord and Savior, Jesus Christ. Then I want to personally send a special Thank You to my one and only true love, Keith D. Samuels, Sr. I could not have come this far without your loving support and prayers.

I also want to acknowledge my children who inspire me to keep going.

Last but not least, a personal "shout out" to every person who spoke into my life and seen my purpose before I believed in myself. Especially to my friend, prayer partner and Sister to heart, Chikita Brown Mann. Words can't express how much I value your anointing and your gift on your life. – *Joyce M. H. Samuels*

Deliverance from Destruction

Joyce M. H. Samuels

"Why can't I stop?" This was the question I asked myself after every time. It was worse than having any other type of addiction. But I just couldn't stop. I kept praying. I asked God to help me stop. I begged and pleaded. I cried. Every time I was finished, I would hide my face in shame. I'm talking about bulimia. I am a recovering bulimic. Yes, this highly educated, saved, preaching, praying and traveling evangelist was bulimic. Now, don't start looking at me funny when you see me, Saints. I had a major issue with emotional eating. I first noticed it around the age of thirteen. During most of my childhood, especially during my foster years, I was called many names. Can I be real with you, reader? Names such as the "b" word, High-Yella Heffa, Dimpled-Butt face, Fat-a**. We get the picture, right? I endured these names for years. I was a very skinny girl while growing up into my teenaged years. I used to hate it. But after I hit puberty, I began to put on weight, and acne was everywhere, even on my chest. I would be so embarrassed. So, then other names surfaced, such as Rat-face, Pimple-pusher, yada-yada. I would feel gross and disgusted. It was already bad enough that I felt awkward in my skin which most young teenagers feel around that age. But, at this point, my body just felt strange to me. Why couldn't I be like all the other normal girls - long hair, smooth skin? It didn't bother me that strangers would call me out my name. It hurt me when my own "family" did. I felt ugly and unattractive.

As a young lady growing into womanhood, I needed constant reminders of my self-esteem. Somebody should had taken the time to tell me how pretty I was, or how smart I was or just tell me how much God loved me and that He made me beautiful. I already had a very rough childhood. My childhood was already traumatic in that I lost my biological mother at the age of seven, lived on the streets, and ate out of trash cans just to get a meal. Surely, I should not have to struggle and fight with my identity as a young woman. I thought "The church is supposed to be a hospital. Isn't that the place where I should feel loved from other saints of the Most High?" I hated myself. I hated my body. I hated who I was and where I came from. I attempted to gain control of my emotions by binge eating. I could eat anything I wanted, then throw it up whenever I wanted. Besides, I had an image I had to uphold, right?! I couldn't get too fat, but then again, I couldn't be too skinny, either. No one knew! That's the insane part. I tortured myself for over 20 years and no one knew. I miscarried six babies, but the doctors could never figure out that I was literally too malnourished to carry a baby full term.

    I would binge on junk food, but would always remember to eat a carrot or some green vegetable so when I see that color during my vomiting episode, I would stop so I could make sure I was saving something "healthy" for the baby. I was putting my body through hell. I was killing myself, literally. I didn't even know that it was a sickness. Didn't know that I needed saving from myself. All I knew - it made me feel like I was in control of my life - or so I thought I was, anyway. I kept telling myself that I could stop whenever I wanted. Lies!!!! It was so bad that I would purchase jars of sauces or jelly, empty out the contents when I got home just so I could throw up at church or even at work and then hide the evidence until I got home or somewhere safe to throw them in the trash container. Singing on the Praise Team - but emotionally sick! Preaching and laying hands, but spiritually dying. Dancing and shouting, but physically punishing myself. What a hypocrite I became!!!! Testifying about how my God was a healer but denying my own healing and concealing my emotional and spiritual illnesses. Every week, I kept promising myself and God that I would stop. But, honestly, I just didn't see anything wrong with it at first. After all, it is my body, right? But, I was very sick.

Let's fast forward to age 29. This is when it got real. I have two healthy sons and just lost another baby girl by miscarriage. I was four months pregnant. This devastated me! I became so angry with God. I blamed Him for everything. How could He allow these things to keep happening to me? What was wrong with me?

Surely, God did not love me. He had forgotten me. Was God even real? I asked myself these questions almost every day. I needed proof. Now granted - I'm already doing damage to my physical body. I was emotionally, spiritually, and physically a mess. What I have learned now about eating disorders is that even though it is manifested as a physical condition, it has an emotional and spiritual origin that stems from corrupted roots. Because of the trauma of molestation, emotional abuse, taunting and rape, the roots of hurt, pain, anger, and self-hatred manifested outwardly into bulimia. The emotional and spiritual bondage had me in a straitjacket.

Proverbs 25:28 reads; "He that hath no rule over his own spirit is like a city that is broken down, and without walls."

Real talk, I had issues! I was broken. But I didn't know how to stop. I was addicted to control. I needed something to control. Just like a drug addict or an alcoholic. I just didn't know how to stop. And to be honest with you - it made me feel good about myself when I did throw up. That's the thing about addictions – they provide temporary highs and then you come crashing down to have to deal with the same issues you are trying to escape from. After each meal, I would wait about thirty minutes then stick my fingers, toothbrush or even a pen down my throat. I felt as though I was accomplishing something every time I emptied my stomach. I felt like I was successful. I felt like I was trying to make all the ones who said that I was nothing a liar. I kept telling myself that I was winning. Sad, right? But it made me feel like I could do what I wanted to do. I felt powerful. It got so bad that I always would carry my "special" toothbrush or pen in my purse.

      One time I almost got caught. We were having a second service at my old church and I was presiding. I ate a cheeseburger for lunch. Beef was very hard to come up after it went down, so I had to take extra care to regurgitate it back up. Just so I didn't choke, I had to sip warm water after each time the food came back up. I got so caught up in what I was doing that church service had already started and they were running around the church building looking for me, including the Pastor. Finally, one of the Ministers banged on the bathroom stall and asked me did I need anything and the church was waiting on me. I was on the knees, bent over the toilet. She looked under the stall and saw that I was throwing up and she began to pray and rebuked my stomach flu. I felt so ashamed! I asked her to go ahead and begin service and apologize to Pastor for me.

Eventually, I came to the hard realization that I needed to be healed from the inside out. But, just like any other addiction, I did not know how to seek for help. I knew scriptures, but was not strong enough to implement them. I knew how to pray, but was weakened by unbelief. I did not know how to apply scripture to my situations. Where was I to go? Who could I talk to? It was not until I was ordered by the courts to attend counseling from the judge due to domestic abuse while finalizing my divorce in my first marriage. For the very first time I finally openly admitted to a total stranger that I was having issues with eating. When I heard the words come out of my mouth, I began to cry. I wept and wept and wept and wept. I felt so relieved but still lost at the same time. That's the first time I told anyone that I needed help. I think I was down to about 110 pounds then. The psychologist promised to get me the help I needed. That's when I finally learned of the medical terminology of the disease. But the crazy thing is, I still didn't stop. It actually got worse. You see, I didn't just need the medical cure, I needed the Blood of Jesus! I needed a divine emotional and spiritual healing. My soul needed healing.

One day I was lying in my bed reading when I received a visitation from the Lord. He began to minister to me. It was similar to being wrapped in a warm, heated blanket of love, compassion, security and peace. And instantly, I surrendered and felt the desire being taking away. I felt full and complete. I felt LIBERATED. I knew I was healed. Healed from bondage and destruction. I truly did not know how sick I was until that visitation. God's love showed me myself. He showed me why I was so angry, so lost and so confused and sad. Most of all, He helped me to accept who I was. I began to see my mother's pain, my father's heartache and it was then that I understood where all my hurt was stemming from. All my hidden, dark childhood secrets started to resurface. But I wasn't afraid anymore. I realized that "hurting people, hurt people." As much as

I didn't like it, I had to deal with the spirit of destruction. My mother's demons were hidden in drugs, prostitution and alcohol. That's what her mother's demons were as well. They died in that. The difference for me was I wanted and sought deliverance.

> Psalms 107:20 reads, "He sent His word, and healed them, and delivered them from their destructions."

I was delivered from my destruction! Glory to God! I was destroying myself. The enemy will use every tool including your past mistakes, your family, your finances and even your own insecurities to cause you to think that you are not worth anything. This form of bondage is running rampant in churches today. We haven't learned how to deal with our toxic emotions. It's time for us to reveal and uncover our own brokenness and to confess to our Savior that we need His delivering power to set us free from ourselves.

"If the son therefore shall make you free; you shall be free indeed." John 8:36

Acknowledgements

This chapter is dedicated to the amazing women who laid the foundation upon which I stand and are part of the fabric of my life: Gloria Pilgrim (Mom), Sheila Pilgrim (Aunt), Hortense Brathwaite and Sandra Durant (teachers); Allison Maria, Kathy Pilgrim-Hall (Sister and Cousin) and LaToya Everett (Sister from another Mister).

I would not be who I am without all of you! Thank you so much for your invaluable wisdom, encouragement and love over the years. - ***Kimberly A. DiStefano***

My Walk with God

Kimberly A. DiStefano

"[1] I will lift up mine eyes unto the hills, from whence cometh my help. [2] My help cometh from the LORD, which made heaven and earth. [3] He will not suffer thy foot to be moved: he that keepeth thee will not slumber. [4] Behold, he that keepeth Israel shall neither slumber nor sleep. [5] The LORD is thy keeper: the LORD is thy shade upon thy right hand. [6] The sun shall not smite thee by day, nor the moon by night. [7] The LORD shall preserve thee from all evil: He shall preserve thy soul. [8] The LORD shall preserve thy going out and thy coming in from this time forth, and even for evermore" (Psalm 121:1-8 KJV).

This scripture was the stabilizing force in my life when I first came to Christ with a made up mind. I had come to Christ many times before but never like that day back in February 2005. That's when I finally came to the end of myself. All the other times I attempted to give my life over to Christ and grant Him permission to have His way with me, the journey ended shortly after it begun. It was short-lived because my bags were overweight and I wasn't ready nor determined enough to unpack them or better yet, leave the bags right where they should have been left; in my past. Not unlike when you're traveling and your bags exceed that 50lb restriction and the airline personnel gives you the choice to 1) take items out of the bag to decrease the weight or 2) you, that bag or both won't get on that flight. Yup, each time I tried, I got left behind the move of God or missed what He was doing because I was distracted and weighed down by my emotional baggage.

When I was finally determined to walk with God, I came to the realization that I needed to develop laser-sharp focus. I needed to keep my mind stayed on Christ and raise my level of thinking from where it was, steeped in carnality, to the high calling of God. It brought to my remembrance Isaiah 55:9, *"For as the heavens are higher than the earth, so are my ways higher than your ways, and my thoughts than your thoughts"*. Hence, my prayers became a plea to God to change my mind, raise my thinking from the bowels of carnality to the unending heights of heaven. After all, how could I rightly walk with God if I did not understand His way of thinking?

How could I reach that heavenly dimension if I didn't understand the blueprint placed before me to navigate? The answer was simple, I couldn't and if I really wanted my mind to mirror that of Christ, there were some things I needed to do. First, I had to stop or turn away from the things I was doing that hindered me from growing mentally in Christ.

To say that my transformation was radical is an understatement. I went all the way to the left and stayed there for a very long time. I completely removed myself from people that were not trying to walk the same path; I completely stopped listening to anything, music, television, conversations, etc., that were not of God. I know it seems extreme and it really was; it needed to be. I wanted to completely saturate myself in the presence of God. I did not want anything contrary to that in my ears. I needed to hear from God and experience Him in a new way. After all, as I shared in the first book, *"Rescued for His Glory"*, I was truly submitting myself to God for the first time ever and if I was going to emerge from this valley better than I went in, ready to serve God and His Kingdom, I needed to clearly hear His instructions for my life. I didn't want His voice to be in competition with the voice of anyone or anything else.

Acknowledging that I was having a "valley" experience was important because I didn't want to miss the reason why I was there by pretending that I wasn't. I wasn't even going to pretend that it was someone else's fault that I was in this particular valley. What good would that do? Not much. I didn't want to focus on anyone else's actions because they were not in that valley with me. Sure, I was a victim but I was a victim of my mind; a prodigal mind that had not come into a full understanding of the power of God and His ways. I couldn't focus on the external enemy when the inner me had been the real sniper, poised to take me out. Additionally, you can't come to God posturing and pretending. Total humility was necessary in order to hear a transformational truth from Him and the absolute truth was what I needed. I had to acknowledge my position in the valley and until I did, uncovering why I was there would be next to impossible. It was a guarantee that I would have stayed there indefinitely or come out not having received the benefit of having been there.

Yes, there is benefit of being in the valley. What you get out of your valley experience depends on what God needs to get out of you. Even as a victim, God shows you a very different view of yourself. So I focused inward. It was no longer important who had done what or why and it was no longer important when innocence was taken advantage of or stolen. Again, what did any of it matter? I needed to FINALLY unpack my emotional baggage because carrying it, as long as I had, almost left me in a state of paralysis. There was no place for embarrassment as I started to unpack that prideful spirit, the spirit of fear, the spirit of low self-esteem and low self-worth, that jezebel spirit, the generational curses and buried underneath them all, was the rejected spirit, which was the one that under-girded and supported all the others. Yup, that one definitely had to go. I unpacked until there were no more strongholds covering and suffocating my spirit man. I broke every chain until I was naked before God, ready to submit to His word, His way, and His will.

There is no experience that can compare to standing humbly and vulnerably before the Lord; but that was only the beginning. Now that I was standing naked before the Lord, I had to be open to receive what He would download into my spirit. I wanted to be absolutely certain that there was nothing left to hinder my transformational journey, so I started to pray,

> "[7]*The law of the Lord is perfect, refreshing the soul. The statutes of the Lord are trustworthy, making wise the simple.* [8]*The precepts of the Lord are right, giving joy to the heart. The commands of the Lord are radiant, giving light to the eyes.* [9]*The fear of the Lord is pure, enduring forever. The decrees of the Lord are firm, and all of them are righteous.* [10]*They are more precious than gold, than much pure gold; they are sweeter than honey, than honey from the honeycomb.* [11]*By them your servant is warned; in keeping them there is great reward.* [12]*But who can discern their own errors? Forgive my hidden faults.* [13]*Keep your servant also from willful sins; may they not rule over me. Then I will be blameless, innocent of great transgression.* [14]*May these words of my mouth and this meditation of my heart be*

pleasing in your sight, Lord, my Rock and my Redeemer." (Psalm 19:7-14)

When you pray this kind of prayer, you have to be open to accept what God shows you about yourself and be ready to make the necessary changes. You have to be okay with the cleansing and deliverance process. It can be painful as you pull back the scabs and start to cleanse your festering wounds. You have to be ready to go as deep as your pain and hurt is rooted. You have to be ready for a spiritual excavation. You have to be ready to do the work, your work. I was ready to do the work. I had already tried it my way and had made a mess of it thus far. I had nothing to lose by relinquishing to God what He created from the beginning of my time.

As I stood naked and vulnerable before God, praying that He would show and remove everything from me that wasn't part of the original package, I started to yearn to know me. I wanted to know God's original thought when He created me. Who did you create me to be Lord? What is my why; my purpose for being in the earth? How can I best serve you Lord and how do I get there? I had no more baggage or chains and

I was ready to move from that stagnant place. I was excited about the possibilities. However, for all my zeal, God spoke to me through the wisdom of my Pastor. He said, "To know you, you first have to know God". I have to admit; it took the wind out of my sails a little bit but not for long. I had not felt this light in a long time so I recalibrated and asked the right question because to get the right answer, you have to ask the right question. So I asked, "How do I go about knowing God?"

As I suspected, there wasn't a one-size-fits-all approach to getting to know God. There are many facets to getting to know God based on what He needs from you and what you need to do for Him. It was all very overwhelming but it was doable. I just needed to be focused and deliberate on a daily basis. There was nothing more important than doing this work because it was the foundation upon which everything else I did and became would stand. So I started to do the work because being made by God is a process:

I Read the Word – Reading the bible can be a daunting task. There are so many versions and then… where do you really begin? Most people want to start at the beginning with Genesis. I tried that, but as I learned from my spiritual leader and from conducting my own research, the Books of John, Ephesians and Romans are great books that lay a solid foundation for individuals new to the Kingdom of God. John gives you the truth of who Jesus was and His ministry. It solidifies your belief that Jesus of Nazareth was Christ, the Son of God, and that believers in Him might have eternal life. Reading the Book of John gave me a sense of purpose because obtaining eternal life was certainly a goal I wanted to achieve. The Book of Romans grounds you in your faith. It tells you that you're justified by faith and not by works. So, I learned quickly that while it was good to work on behalf of God, my faith was the catalyst that would have God move on my behalf. He did it for the woman with the issue of blood (Matthew 9:20-22), he did it for the Canaanite woman (Matthew 15:21-28), he did it for Zacchaeus (Luke 19:1-10) and so many others, I knew without a shadow of a doubt, He could and would do it for me! Finally, the Book of Ephesians helped me to understand my place in the earth. It was necessary to fulfill my role in the Kingdom. It taught me that I was predestined before the foundation of the world and sealed by the Holy Spirit. Ephesians gave me solid direction on how I should live morally and ethically as a follower of Christ.

I Developed a Prayer Life – So many people say these cute and cliché lines such as, "There's nothing like the power of prayer." and I wholeheartedly agree. However, the power is not in the words you speak, the power is in praying the Word; believing in the promises of God, and what you learn about Him and who He is as you begin to read and understand the Word. Talking to God and learning how to sit and listen to him was paramount to my journey out of the valley. Waiting for a response, knowing that even no response was a response and I just needed to trust Him and His infinite wisdom was part of the process. It was during this part of my valley experience that I started to develop fruit. It wasn't strange fruit but it was finally fruit of the spirit. It was patience, peace, joy. It was a beginning and I learned what it meant to relinquish everything to my Father, knowing that whatever His plan was for me, it was 100%

better than any plan I could come up with on my best day!

I Worshipped with a Body of Like-Minded Believers – It is when you are in the valley that you need a body of like-minded believers the most. Isolating yourself from the encouragement and edification of the Saints will leave you vulnerable to an attack from the enemy. During my valley experience, my church family was the most encouraging and supportive. They understood what I needed and when I needed it; they knew when to pray for me, they knew when to exhort me, they knew when I needed some spiritual toughness and they knew when to just smile. The bible says, *"let us consider how to stimulate one another to love and good deeds,_not forsaking our own assembling together, as is the habit of some, but encouraging one another; and all the more as you see the day drawing near"* (Hebrews 10:24-25). All of us are essential and necessary to the spiritual development of each other. My church family understood that even in my valley, growth, positive movement toward being ready to walk in my purpose was necessary, and they held me accountable to exactly that. They saw potential and promise even in the midst of my valley and they loved me through it all. They were like-minded; so they understood that the process was a critical part of God preparing me for greater purpose in and for Him. We were all in one phase or another of our process and needed each other as God directed to ensure successful transformation. Again, the buds of additional fruit started to emerge. I learned to love without conditions and limits, to be gentle and kind. I was truly starting to blossom.

I Became the Change God Wanted to See – In 2008, Israel and New Breed penned lyrics to a song on his, *"Deeper Level"* album. There was a segment on the album entitled, *"Deeper Prayer",* orated by Darlene Zschech. It said, *"Father I want to get to heaven with a life poured out. Not with a life that looks perfect; Father I don't want it to just look good, I want it to be good".* This spoke to a personal and intimate relationship with God and at this leg of my journey, this prayer was exactly how I was feeling. It was exactly what I was saying to God. I was so in love with my Father and who He was to me that I wanted to be everything that I should be for Him. It wasn't about perfection; it was about applying all the principles I had been learning from the moment I checked my bags filled to the brim with negative emotions and feelings. I wanted for everything on my inner parts to be good. I wanted to be the bearer of good fruit. It was important to me that all the studying and praying and fellowshipping I embarked on was not just an intellectual pursuit. It was more about a heart transplant that could recreate mind transformation. It was really about creating a sustainable relationship with God. I was finding my voice and at last, it was coming from a place that was totally submitted to God, His will, His way, without question. It was at this point that I recognized the remaining fruit of the spirit beginning to emerge, self-control, goodness and faithfulness. I was well on my way out of the valley.

Many people think that doing the work is hard and it is, but maintaining what you've worked so hard to accomplish is where the true work really begins. It is so easy to lose the humility you acquired in your valley because you successfully made your way out of one specific valley. Making your way out of one valley does not mean you will not encounter more. It prepares you to better navigate the other valleys you will encounter on your Kingdom journey but you can only do that by maintaining the principles you find and adopt in the valley.

Reading the Word, developing a prayer life and worshipping with other believers are the foundational principles of Kingdom living but we need to develop a growth mindset if we are going to continue learn and know God beyond what He does. The growth mindset delves into why He does what He does. When we develop that growth mindset, we learn that we have to be willing to allow God to move us out of our comfort zone. The danger of becoming comfortable with the status quo is the risk of falling right back into that old mindset because new challenges you in a different way.

The desire for positive and sustainable transformation has to come from within. You have to want it! You have to be willing to do whatever is necessary to attain it and you definitely cannot do the minimum and expect maximum results. God is certainly not a minimalist and for that - I am grateful! We have to disconnect from soul ties that don't positively nurture or encourage Christ centered living and we have to remain teachable and consistently conduct quality control checks to ensure that the fruit growing within you is actually from the Holy Spirit or not contaminating good fruit in its infancy. We can't rely on our spiritual leaders for inspirational messages because inspiration alone does not inspire change. Inspiration should birth an internal desire and motivation to change because people can give you the tools and teach you how to use them but you have to desire to pick them up and apply them accurately to the right life situations, asking the right person the right questions as appropriate. Anything less, will result in a return to that fixed mindset; fixed on any and everything other than God and His purpose for creating yours.

By now, you are wondering what anything I said had to do with Psalm 121. It had everything to do with that scripture! I could not have successfully come out of the valley without keeping my eyes, my heart and my mind stayed on Christ. I stood solidly on the promises that God would never leave me nor forsake me no matter how difficult my valley seemed or the transformation process became. In those tough and defining valley moments, I took comfort in the knowledge that the Lord would keep me that He would watch over me regardless to what I was going through. With this knowledge, I didn't have to look to the left nor did I have to look to the right because I knew God had all my bases covered if I just stayed focused on Him. Because I decided to trust Him in my valley, I just needed to follow His instructions because He had the blueprint that was specific to me. He understood the end result so I just trusted him to guide and guard me through the process.

My valley experience enabled me to find my voice. It equipped me with the tools and tolerance to walk into and in purpose bearing good fruit and cross pollenating other's God put in my path. A transformative God experience changed my vocal patterns from that of pain to that of purpose and promise! I dare you to try God in your valley. The voice you discover and develop there will create a lasting echo of God's glory and goodness. What are you waiting for? Let's go!

Acknowledgements

This chapter is dedicated to God! – *Serrica Jackson*

Damaged Inside and Out

Serrica Jackson

I always thought of family as loving and happy; where we would bond and come together as one and where the mother and father worked to take care of the children. Of course, there would be discipline, but I never thought I would experience the horrible things I experienced once I left the dream family I once had.

Let's go back to the beginning when things were so loving and peaceful. My mother had me at a young age so my oldest brother and I had to go live with our great grandma because my grandma worked two jobs in order to support us and my mother attempted to go back to school after having me. My aunt, a teenager herself, had to stop being a teenager so she could help my mother with us.

As a child, I thought this was how a family was supposed to be. Don't get me wrong, my grandma was an amazing provider for us. She showed us how a grandma was supposed to love her grandbabies, so I truly appreciate her in so many ways. She will forever have my heart.

One day my LIFE changed for the worst. I felt like my heart had been ripped out.

It was a normal day like any other. My oldest brother and I were outside playing with mud pies. Momma was in the house cooking dinner and papa was working at the barbershop. Little did we know that this would be the day that would change our lives forever.

It was time for Papa to finish up at the barbershop and come home for the night. He entered, as always, with treats for us with love in his eyes. As we were sitting down for dinner, we heard a knock at the door. It was my mother saying it was time for us to go. My mama asked where she was taking us and my mother said we were moving to another state and that we would visit in the summer, which never happened.

We noticed our Papa jumped up to see what was wrong with our mama. All we could hear from the kitchen was crying and begging for my mother not to take us. We finally got up from the table to go into the living room and my mama knelt down beside us telling us to pack our things so we could go with our mother. We were crying and screaming; clearly we didn't want to go. We had never seen our mama and papa cry before and to hear them BEG her to allow us to stay really hurt me, still to this day. My mother just kept making excuses on why we couldn't stay. My mama just kept saying that we were fine and that we weren't in the way. She said that they loved having us there but my mother's mind was already made up. She was taking us with her. We just cried and cried and cried until we fell asleep in the car. When we woke up, we were in another state and it was COLD. At this point, we were asking where our mama and papa were but we never got an answer.

We were now all settled in this cold city with no real family other than the people we came up there with. For a while, everything was fine until one bad, bad day when we had to sleep in the car because my mother and her boyfriend were fighting about something. I, being the outspoken one, could never understand how we went from being in a warm apartment to sleeping in a cold car. While sitting in the car my mother remembered that she left something in the house but she was too scared to get out the car to get it. She made my brother get out of the car to get it. While we waited, the MONSTER came out to the car. He reached inside the car, turned the car off and pulled out her keys. My mother pulled out a spare key from her bag and turned the car back on. He just looks at her and shakes his head. My brother ran out of the house into the cold car with us.

We had days when we starved because he wouldn't allow us to come into his house. Then, there were days we would sneak into the house when he was gone with the other two children. We couldn't understand why we were being treated so differently from the other kids; why he didn't like us? What did we do? We were only six and five years old. We shouldn't have been worried about things like that. Finally, we were allowed to come back in the house after four months of being in the cold. Then came another brutal attack on my mother right in front of us. We were getting ready for school and about to leave when he said something to our mother. When she responded he dragged her from the living room all the way back to their room. He pulled her up against the wall and told her he would kill her and us. He then hit her in the face with a gun. Blood was everywhere. I was crying so bad that he yelled at me to "shut the HELL UP NOW"!

My mother got up and started getting herself together so we could walk to school. As we were leaving out my mother tells me, the one in kindergarten, to call the police once I got to school but I never did. At the end of the day we waited for our mother to pick us up but the policeman came in to get us instead. I would not allow myself or my brother to leave because I wasn't sure if the MONSTER was trying to trick us; he would play those type of tricks on us just to whoop us. So, I told the police I was taught not to go with anyone and that also meant police officers. He told me that my mom was outside but I still said we could not go. "We will get our butts whooped really badly if we go." He called another policeman and told him what I said. The other officer came in with our mother. We ran up to her when we saw her. The police officer told her I wouldn't come out with him and she said, "Yes, he hits on them." That day we were placed in a shelter. We stayed in the shelter for a few days and then we were right back at the Monster's house. On top of that, she tells us she is having a baby so now we had to move to another apartment.

This time, we moved from Washington DC to Maryland in a one-bedroom apartment with two adults, four children, and a baby on the way. Things were fine. We were doing family things together like going to the Wharf to get crabs, going to the playground and the zoo. I was sure things were going to stay that way until one day, while in the van, my mom states that she was going into labor. We all d rove to the hospital but we had to go home without our mom which I didn't like at all.

When we got back home we took our baths and got ready for bed, then he tells us he had to go back to the hospital with our mother. I was left in charge of my siblings. Once he got back that night I felt him touching me. I woke up with his fingers in between my legs touching my private area. He then made me get up and get in the bed with him, the same bed he shared with my mother. I remember hearing myself saying, "NO THIS IS NOT RIGHT. PLEASE DON'T MAKE ME." But he still pulled me in the room. He made me watch porn. He rubbed on my legs, back; rubbed me down with lotion while my other little sister was sleeping in the bed. The whole time my mother was in the hospital he had me laying in their bed, which was so weird; talking to me like I was an adult. Then, once my mother came home with the new baby he would act like nothing had happened but I knew what was happening. I just w anted things to STOP. I'm thinking this is not going to happen again. I was so WRONG. While I was sleeping on the couch with my siblings, I felt something HEAVY on me so I moved around to get comfortable but I could not. I opened my eyes and it was him playing with my private area. I get up, he pushed me back down. Then someone started moving around in the bed so he ducked down on the floor while I'm trying to get him off me. He slapped me in the face. By then I was crying. As he was doing all these different things to me, my mother was in another room with the baby. I remember a particular day like it was yesterday. I was sitting behind the couch with one of my siblings. He came out his room and sat on the couch. He put his hands under my shorts but I pulled away from him and gave him a look.

The abuse got worse as time went on. We moved into a two bedroom and a den. I started to notice my mother was not home a lot. She didn't have a job so I would ask her where she was going and why she was gone so much. This gave him more power to continue hurting me and beating on my brother. I would be sleep and he would come into the room that I shared with his daughters in his underclothes to wake me up so I could put my mouth on him. I would say "NO" or fight him off and he would slap and punch me. He even cut me one day in the middle of my chest because I wouldn't do something he wanted me to do. He would make me jerk him off then he would ejaculate in my mouth. He would pee in my mouth and wouldn't let me spit it out. He would choke me. He would always threaten me by saying that he would kill me and no one would know he did it. I just never understood why I was going through as much as a child.

I remember at the age of 8, riding home from picking up my little sister from school. We got out of the car and a lady, who lived in our building, started running towards my mom, punching her. I jumped on the lady's back and started punching her and screaming for her to get off of my mother. Another lady we knew came running out of the building, pulling the lady off of my mother. I saw him across the street watching while all of this was going on. The next day our mother had a blood clot in her eye and her eye was black. I just couldn't believe he just let this happen to my mother. I HATED him more and more because what if that lady would have killed my mother? Who was going to take care of us? So many times, I thought of running away from all the pain I was feeling. There would be times I would cry wondering why these things were happening to us.

I would be blamed for so many things. For instance, one day we were all outside playing. I went back in the house to use the bathroom but before I went into the house my mother was coming out the building. She told me that she would be back and to keep an eye on my siblings until she returned. I said okay. My mom started walking up the street and I went in the house. When I came back outside all I heard was my sister crying and my mother running back down the street. I ran into the street where I saw my little sister under a car, my mother crying, the MONSTER cussing and the person who hit her saying he was SORRY and that he didn't see her run out in the street. The monster is yelling at me asking why I wasn't watching her. I was trying to explain that I was in the house using the bathroom and that I didn't know she was going to run in the street behind mom. He beat me so bad that day and he molested me the whole night. I wish I was the one who was hit by that car and not my sister. I just wanted to get away from all the pain my body and mind was feeling. He would make us fight together and if we didn't fight he would beat us so bad our skin would bleed.

When I was in the 4th grade I drew a picture of a male pig (no original pig) but a pig with a penis hanging down and I'm not sure how my 4th-grade teacher saw the picture but she sent me home with a note for my mother. The very next day, my teacher had a meeting with my mother and showed her the picture. I was thinking that my mom was going to talk to me once I got home to find out what made me draw this picture. Nope, it didn't happen like that at all. I got home and the picture was on the refrigerator. I didn't know what to do but I wanted to run far away until the picture was gone. I knew right then and there I was in BIG TROUBLE and when that door opened it was him, with the belt and he just beat my little butt so bad my skin was bleeding and I ran out the room, tripped and chipped my front tooth on a wagon. I just screamed and screamed that I wanted my grandmother.

I started to notice his behavior was starting to get odd. More and more people would be at our house and our house smelled different. We used to all cook together, bake cookies and cakes, go to the Wharf to get crabs, play at Anacostia Park but that all came to an end. We never understood why since we loved to do those things. Those were the only things that made us feel like a close family.

His sisters, nieces, and nephews would come to visit and he would act all nice like nothing was going on but I knew it was all a front. I would always wonder if their dad ever touched his sisters inappropriately and if that is why he was doing me that way or even if he had done anything bad to his own sisters.

One day we sat down at this "so called" family meeting for the MONSTER to stand up and say, "Guess what? MOMMY IS HAVING ANOTHER BABY." I said to myself, "Great, another person for me to take care of." I just walked away with so much disappointment in my eyes. I was hurt, sad and upset. I couldn't understand why she kept having babies with the MONSTER. Doesn't she know he's hurting me? I cried to myself that whole day because I couldn't believe it. Everything may have seemed normal but it wasn't. I was still being molested and getting hit and so was my big brother. He would hit us with bats, extension cords, and his hands. He would punch us in the chest, make us do pushups. He would ball his fists up just to hit us in the head.

We were living in a two-bedroom apartment with a den. I was sharing a room with my sisters, which never bothered him because he would still come in the room and touch on me whether I was asleep or woke. I remember one night we were all in my brother's room watching television. I got up to go to my room because I wasn't feeling well, so I fell off to sleep. When I woke up the MONSTER was between my legs, I'm crying, I'm moving, I'm asking him to stop doing these things to me. I remember while my mother was having his third daughter, he would make me wear her nightgown. I would never forget the d ay he would always try to get me to take a shower with him but I would never do it so he would make me wash him up. Then he would make me take a shower then give me directions to come in his room after I was done which I would never do. so he would have to come look for me and he would say I thought I told to come in my room I see you don't like to listen and slap me across my face.

He started to notice that I started having my period, which would really be the only time he wouldn't mess with me. On top of that, I started getting "bee stings" in my shirt (my little chest is growing now). My mother is healed from having the baby and was she back hanging in the streets all hours of the night. I even ask her, once, if I could go with her and she would always tell me NO. Some nights I would sit up and wait for my mother so I could ask her why does she always leave at night; I knew she wasn't going to work or was she. I could never understand how she didn't know this man was hurting me every night. I just never knew what he was going to do to me next so I just started locking the door. I didn't matter, somehow he would always end up in my room either sucking on my bee stings or fingering me or making me put my mouth on him. By now I was tired and the next day I was planning to run away from home. I have my things packed and ready to go when my mother tells me she was going out of town because something was going on with my grandmother. I begged her to take me with her. But she didn't. She didn't take any of the other children and I couldn't understand why she would leave me with this SICK MONSTER. Once she left he told me that now he had me all to his self. I just went into the room and cried my little eyes out.

    One day, while my mother was out of town, I walked to the pay phone to call her. I look up and the MONSTER is standing right in front of me. My mom asked me something about my dad so I'm trying my hardest to speak in code language so that he would not hear me. All I could see was this mad look on his face. When I hung up he questioned me about what my mom asked me and what I said to her. He didn't like that I would not give him the answers he was looking for. The last thing he said before I got on the school bus was, "Someone will pay for this." I thought about those words the whole day in school. I was scared when it was time to go home because I didn't know what that meant.

Some nights I plotted on how I was going to kill myself at the age of 10. I just wanted to escape everything; I was so tired of the abuse and I was tired of not having a mother or father. It felt as if no one loved me. He would blow crack smoke in my face; he even asks me if I wanted to try it. I said, "Heck NO! I'm a kid." Our house was the crack house and I couldn't understand why every evening after school there would be all these people in our house. While my mother was away in Georgia she would call our neighbor's phone so we could talk to her and I would ask her when she was coming home but all she would say was, "in a few days." To me, it felt like a lifetime. She would ask me if things were okay there but I couldn't really tell her because he was always there.

I would come back to the house and go into my room and cry, my siblings never knew what was going on. They never understood why I would have my crying moments. One particular day, we were all outside playing and I had to use the bathroom. I brought one of my sisters in the house, which is something I always did. I hurried and used the bathroom before he could notice we were in the house. We rushed into the kitchen to get something to drink when I hear the monster so I pulled my sister back and we went back outside to play. My brother told me that the MONSTER wanted me to come in the house because the baby was crying. I can't even remember what I was feeling that day but I will say this, I was scared out my mind because I wasn't sure what was about to happen. I finally get up to our door, I place my hand on the doorknob and as I open the door I didn't hear anything. As I got in the house and shut the door, he jumped out from behind and picked me up. He started to kiss me but I pulled away. He then put his hands around my neck; I'm crying and crying for him to let me go. So he finally does and then out of nowhere he tells me to do him a favor. I still haven't gotten myself together, so I'm crying even more now. He pulls out his private area and tells me to put my mouth on it and I start to cry even more.

Once he figured out that I was not about to do what he wanted me to do, he grabs me by my neck and he pulls me closer to him. I still didn't open my mouth but he forced me to. I didn't see the smack to the face coming until I felt my face burning. I'm crying more now so then he yells at me to SHUT THE HELL UP NOW. He then started pumping his private area in and out my mouth; sperm came out of his private area and he wanted me to swallow it but I spit it out so he slaps me across my face again. He then picks me up by my neck and told me if I every spit it out again, he would kill me. "Now, go in the bathroom and clean yourself up child." I ran so fast to the bathroom and locked the door. I just cried and cried. That day, I scrubbed and scrubbed until I felt like my skin was burning. I just wanted to get scrub away everything that just happens to me. My mother comes in the house, as if she had not been away for so long, and asked what was wrong with me. I said, "Nothing at all." "Then why you not outside?" I told her that I didn't feel good and all she said to me was to lay down take a nap. In my little head, all I can think was, "Where were you all of this time while he was hurting me?" She just has to know that he was doing these things to me.

By now it's laundry day so we all packed up all our dirty clothes to take to the big laundromat, everyone except him. We all were dragging our clothes across the street; it felt so good to have our mom to ourselves without him being there to make us feel scared to do or say anything. When we got back home with our clean clothes, I was in the hall closet putting up towels, rags and sheets when he comes out his room and he grabs my private area while my mother was in the living room. I gave him this dirty look and he gave me this deviously grin as if he wanted to hit me upside my head. I went to my room and then heard my mother calling me. She wanted to know where I had been that whole time and asked what was wrong with me. Because he was standing in the kitchen looking and listening, I just told her nothing. Once all clothes were put up, my mother made me come in the bathroom with her. She laid me across her lap and smells my girl parts which I never understood. I asked her why she always did that but she would never give me a reason, she just did it.

When he wasn't molesting me, he would beat on my older brother for everything he did. I become his shield, his voice, his backbone. I would jump in the way whenever he would hit my brother; I will never forget the day my brother was horsing around like kids do and he got so mad. He came in the living room with this big wooden stick and he swung it. I jumped in the way and fell down. He swung it again and hit my brother in his face. My arm was broken and my brother's face had a big knot on it. My mother did nothing to help us. She just allowed him to do whatever he wanted to us. That exact same day I decided that he would pay for what he did to my brother. I hated my mother more and more for the things we had to endure.

Then the day came that changed my whole world for the worse. My mother gets a call saying that my great grandma was in the hospital and it was urgent that she come back home. She came over and told my big brother that our mama was in the hospital. I begged my mother to take me with her and she said yes. That night I fell asleep in the dining room area. I rolled over that night and he was there rubbing my private area thru my shorts. I jumped and screamed. He slapped me across my face so hard and said you know you like this so stop fighting it. That next day, I couldn't wait to get away from HELL. I even begged my mother to let my older brother go with us but he wasn't allowing both of us to leave so I left with my mom. I thought about my brother the whole time I was gone. I wondered what was going on and whether he had been hurt. It hurt me so badly that my big brother wasn't with us when we buried our mama and he was crushed as well.

Well, we went back to living in the normal hell hole we were in before we left. We get a knock on the door from the neighbor telling the monster that my mom was on the phone. He goes over and comes back to inform us that our mother was in JAIL and that he will go tomorrow to see why she is in there. The next day he went to the jail and found out she was there for some stealing checks. I just kept saying WHY, WHY and crying so hard the whole day because I couldn't believe what was going on and why these things kept happening to me. That night, he woke me up out my sleep to tell me he needs me to HELP get my mother out of JAIL. I told him I'm just a kid, what could I do? He goes to the window in my room, points out the window to a gold car with four men in it. He said they were going to help get my mother out of jail but they were looking for three things. He points to my mouth, my private area, and my butt and I flat out told him NO! I told him she got herself in this mess and she need to get her stuff out this mess I'm just a KID who supposed to be a KID. He just kept trying to convince me this is the right thing to do and he would be in the closet with his shotgun if anything bad happens. So he goes to the closet and pulls me into a said I'm going to show all the things you will have to do. So he took off all his clothes and laid on my floor, pulls me down and pulls off my clothes. I'm fighting him but of course, he wins. Now I'm laying on top of him crying my eyes out when he starts to rub his penis on my butt and on my vagina. I felt him trying to put his penis inside me and I'm fighting and crying because now it is in. I just cried and cried until it was over.

There was a particular day I was getting myself and my little sisters things together so we could spend the night over my friend house. So I happen to walk around the corner to ask my friend a question I happen to see the MONSTER hit her but no one heard or seen me coming. How could this child still want to hang around me knowing that my step -father was hitting her like that? I knew I had to tell someone what was going on because it wasn't fair that she was being abused. So, we got on the bus that next morning for school and as we were about to leave out, my mother came walking through the door. She told us to have a good day and that she would see us once we got out of school.

Once I was on the bus someone yelled out, "Your father is hitting on her!" I was so embarrassed. That was the day I decided to tell someone about the abuse I was facing on a daily basis. I told my principal what was happening and why I didn't want to go home. She called social services. Little did anyone know that on that day it would be the last day any of them would see me again. After years of total torture, physical, and mental abuse, I truly can say I have survived, overcame and through the

Grace of God, I'm thankful He allowed me to live to be able to tell my story to advocate for others! There is more to my story and one day I will be able to tell it all. No child should every experience what I went through as a child.

Acknowledgement

I would like to thank my Awesome husband Sylvester Jackson, for praying with me, always supporting me, keeping me uplifted, motivated and inspiring me to always be my best. God Blessed me with one of his greatest creations. I would like to thank Joyce Samuels for allowing me to be a part of this collaboration to inspire others to keep God first and pray. To my children Sylvester, IV and David thank you for showing me what unconditional love really is. – *Evelyn M. Jackson*

God's Timing Not My Own

Evelyn M. Jackson

My story started in 1995 when my then fiancé and I decided to have a baby. He thought that I couldn't have children because it hadn't happened quickly enough. I wasn't worried, within four months we were expecting our first child.

Our son was born healthy on November 3, 1996, three weeks past his due date. We were so happy! I thought this was it - one and I'm done! I chose not to have a tubal ligation since he wanted another child. We married in August, 1998. In 1999 we thought we were pregnant again but it was a false alarm. Little did I know this would be the beginning of my testimony.

In November of 2000, we found out that we were expecting our 2nd child only, however, I miscarried early on in the pregnancy. I thought to myself, "Why? I am a good mother Lord, why?" We decided to try again. It never took long to conceive but I would miscarry soon afterward. I started questioning myself and my relationship with God. I wondered why so many others who didn't take care of or even want children were able to have a perfectly normal pregnancy, but not me. I so desperately wanted another child, but during each pregnancy, I would become so sick that I would have to be hospitalized and then ultimately, miscarry.

    I had a wonderful support system that tried to keep me encouraged. I became so determined to have another baby but I was reminded that my timing and God's timing may not always be one in the same. I kept trying in 2002, I miscarried twice, once in August and the other in October. That August we were so excited! We finally were able to hear our baby's heartbeat. We thought, "This is it! We are going to make it!" But it was just not meant to be. I was heartbroken. There were people asking why I kept trying and then others who encouraged me to continue praying about it.

I was at an appointment when the radiologist performed a sonogram and could no longer find my baby or hear a heartbeat. She ran from the room almost in tears. A few minutes later, the lead doctor came in and delivered the news; my baby was gone. I screamed out so loud. I was devastated. My husband and son were in the waiting room. They went to get my husband to help me. I was ready to give up but my sister and sister-in-law would keep me lifted in positive prayer. My sister-in-law told me not to give up. She had been through her own miscarriages and gave birth to 2 beautiful baby girls. We returned to my OB/GYN's office, who told me what to expect. I got home and the spotting started. I passed this baby like a menstrual cycle. It felt as if I was holding and flushing my baby down the toilet. I was heartbroken to say the least. My doctor told me that as soon as it passed we could try again. I was so determined at the point to keep trying at all cost. My mother asked why I was trying to kill myself. She said if she could carry our baby herself, she would.

That October 2002, during the scare of the beltway sniper case, I discovered I was pregnant. Again,

I miscarried. For the first time, I had to have a D&C procedure. That same day my husband's friend was the final victim to be killed by the snipers. While lying there watching the news and waiting for the procedure, I couldn't help but ask God why these two lives were being taken.

In June 2003, I was speaking with a nurse from my insurance company who referred me to Dr. Kevin Lewis of Georgetown Hospital in Washington DC. She said he is at the top of his game with high risk pregnancies. By this time I had miscarried 4 times and felt I had nothing to lose. I called and scheduled an appointment to meet with Dr. Lewis. I went, answered a series of questions and underwent a series of test. Some had been done before by a specialist I had previously seen. He told us to begin trying again. He determined I had a protein S deficiency which means I abnormally clotted and the clot was suffocating the sack. It would attack the sack because it was a foreign substance to my body. However, after all of that, I once again miscarried.

Determination really kicked in after that. I prayed long and hard. I asked God how I would know if it's His will for me to have another child. I prayed to be able to have this child that my husband and I so wanted.

In July of 2004 I heard God speaking to me, He said, "The time is now." I told my husband that if we are going to do this, it's now or never. In August, we took a trip to Hershey Park. After two rides I felt it, the little life growing in me. I looked at my husband and said "Oh yeah, were pregnant." We were happy, although we were not ready to tell anyone. We finally told my sister that I was going to the doctor and we knew I was pregnant. She said she was praying for this baby to make it. We had to tell everyone because, like all the other pregnancies, I was sick with hyperemesis. I went to see Dr. Lewis who confirmed the pregnancy. I told him my due date would be April 25th and sure enough, when he did the sonogram, my due date was April 26th. Dr. Lewis said I was the first patient to be that accurate with a due date. At 7 weeks pregnant I was hospitalized with nausea and vomiting again. I was told that my best chances were to have a pic line put in for medications.

On September 22nd, I had the procedure done. Sadly, my sister-in-law, had passed away the night before. But there was something about her passing that convinced me that my baby was going to make it into this world. After being placed on bed rest for the duration of my pregnancy, I still was facing an uphill journey. In late October I had to be hospitalized again for several days. Upon my release, I had another appointment for my triple screen. I received a call 2 days later from Dr. Lewis asking that I come in to the office to review some, not so favorable, test results. I was informed that my baby was showing signs of Down Syndrome. I hung up and cried. I called my husband and my sister who is one of David's Godmothers and told them the news. My sister told me that it was okay. It was still our baby and we would love him or her regardless. I knew she was right. I talked to God and said, "Lord, I asked you for a healthy baby and I know that is what you will give me." I wiped those tears away and claimed that in Jesus' name I would birth a healthy baby. When I went in for my appointment Dr. Lewis checked and everything was fine. That day we discovered we were expecting a new baby boy. We called big brother first and told him the great news! He wanted a brother. We then called my mother who had asked to name him. She said, "Now, all we have to do is wait for the arrival of Blessed David Isaiah." We were all so happy knowing, that after all the miscarriages and trials, we were finally awaiting the arrival of our special miracle.

At an appointment in December, I was told by Dr. Lewis that he was leaving Georgetown and wanted me to follow him. I declined and was transferred to the Chief of OB, Dr. Collea. That January, I saw Dr. Collea and asked for a labor induction date of April 11th. Of course he declined saying, "Mommy, we will let nature take its course." I agreed but after many other months of sickness I was still looking to be induced April 11th. Our special bundle of blessing was being celebrated at a baby shower where we received so many gifts and out pours of love. On April 9th, I was in so much pain, I couldn't walk. The pressure was so bad I cried for two days. I prayed and said, "Lord I know you don't make mistakes but this is a lot to bear." I knew whatever it was - God would receive all the Glory for His works.

On April 10th, I went to the hospital late that Sunday night. They kept me over night and in the morning, on April 11th, they decided to induce. I was so happy! We were coming the end and ready to see our miracle. Later that day, Dr. Collea came in and said I wasn't dilated and the baby wasn't in danger. He planned to send me home later. That afternoon, I went for a sonogram and was told that our baby was in a breach position. So now I was facing delivery by C-section. I asked the Lord, "Why me again?" After all of this, they now determine that my baby was in the correct position. My resident, Dr. Isaiah, said they were still going to send me home. I can help you if you like. He broke my water and April 11th my baby boy was born.

During the entire 9 months, I continued to ask God how I can love another child as much as I loved my oldest. After going through all the sickness, all the pain and everything else, I realized God was sending me my answers. Once you see how much pain and how many sacrifices you are willing to make for this child, you will have experience the love I have for you; unconditional love. God is always on time, no matter what we think or how we feel, He has a ram in the bush. Don't give up or give in. Continue to pray and wait for God's timing and not our own.

Acknowledgements

There are four very special people that I would like to acknowledge and they are; Minister Barbara Mack, Deacon Dennis Mack, Deacon Lowell Philson and Pastor James M. Hillian.

These four people played a big part of my being where I am today. They loved me while I was in my valley experience and prayed me out of the valley.

My mom Minister Mack, consistently showed tough love to me, even though I did not always like what she had to say. She consistently prayed for me. I often think that the reason she can pray so good, is because I kept her on her knees while I was in my valley experience.

My step-dad Deacon Mack was and is concerned about my soul being right with the Lord He is and was a road model for me. I have never heard him say anything negative. When I would make comments, he would always tell me, "it will be alright little girl." When I was in my valley experience, he could have turned his back on me, but he chose to love me from the valley to life.

My brother-in-law Deacon Philson has inspired me down through the years. Watching him as a young fellow playing the guitar and praising God is inspiring to me. He and I talk and in every conversation, I get some preaching out of him. While in my valley experience, he never turned away from me. If I called him, he would pick up the phone and talk. He has a great anointing on his life and because I never thought he did anything wrong, I have always looked up to him, even though he is younger than me. Watching him and his lifestyle, helped me to not want to be in the streets, but be in the church.

My previous Pastor was Pastor Hillian. This Pastor prayed for me week after week for fifteen long years. Not one time did he tell me to stop getting in the prayer line. Not one time did he say anything negative to me. I loved to hear him preach as the anointing on his life was helping me to want to come to church, even if I had been up all night getting high. He and I talked a lot and I found him to be a man of God. Once I became clean, he opened his heart to hear what I had to say about anything. He always provided me with nuggets. Those nuggets helped me to stay focused on getting to where God was taking me. The love that he showed me while in my valley experience, helped me to come out of the valley and stay out. – ***Valerie Johnson-Philson***

The Power of Deliverance

Valerie Johnson-Philson

I thought living a drug free life would be a big challenge. I soon found out that being addicted to crack cocaine was just a mind thing. I have had some down days but not to the extent that I thought it would be.

Shortly after I was delivered from crack cocaine, my mom told me she had breast cancer. Because I had only been clean for a short time, I just knew I would relapse. I was always told that when an addict goes through stress, drama or hurtful situations they could relapse. To my surprise, I had no urge to use again. That ordeal was my confirmation; God had delivered me from drugs. I prayed and asked God not to take my mom; to give me some time with her; time that I missed while using crack cocaine from the age of twenty to the age of thirty-five. Having an addiction did not allow me the opportunity to have a relationship with my family because all I wanted to do was get high.

I rededicated my life to the Lord and became active in church. I sang in the choir and ushered for a long time. This kept me busy because I had to attend practice, attend usher board meetings, as well as, attend Bible Study, Sunday school, Sunday morning worship and other services. Being faithful to these ministries kept my mind focused on serving the Lord. I seldom missed any services. When the church doors were opened I would be front and center, striving to get to where God wanted to take me.

A few years later, the Lord called me into the ministry. It was funny because I was not sure at first, but He also showed the first lady of the church that I was called to preach the gospel. When the Lord called me into the ministry, the Pastor had me to conduct services on Friday nights. I did that for a while and then Friday night services faded out because of low attendance.

Attending church every time the doors opened and changing my friends was the key to my remaining drug free. Once I was delivered, I did not hang out with the same people. I remember one of the drug dealers I used to deal with coming to my house on several occasions to see if his services were needed. I was strong enough to let him know that I was delivered. Eventually, he realized that it was a waste of time for him to come over and he stopped showing up.

My mother, Minister Barbara Mack, played a big role in my ability to stay clean. My mom regularly and consistently prays for me. Whenever I would come in contact with my mom and I was high, I could actually see the hurt on her face. I was so messed up. My mom changed her house locks so that I would not be able to get into her house. My feelings were hurt, but looking back, I understand that she did not know what I might do and she did not want me coming in and out of her home. My mom once said that I looked as if I were dead. I was 90 pounds and walking around with dry, dusty looking skin. My feelings were hurt when my mom said that to me, but it also helped me to become sick and tired of being high. It wasn't long after that I received my deliverance. Still, until this day, my mom continues to pray for me and my family. That is what keeps me going, knowing she is in my corner.

During my addiction, I stayed at the pawn shop pawning my jewelry; children's games; bikes; VCR and any electronics I had in the house to include my televisions. I would sell my food stamps instead of using them to buy food for my children. Some months, I would spend $100 for the house and sale the rest, as I was more concerned with getting a hit than feeding my children.

My grandparents Edward and Louise Johnson, who are both deceased, enabled me a lot. They made sure my children had something to eat, even if it was not what they wanted. My grandparents made sure my children had coats and clothing for school. I would always make up an excuse as to why I need money and my grandparents would make sure I had money. They never asked where my money was and that made me happy. They never knew I was spending my money and food stamps for drugs and the money I got from them on drugs.

My mom once told me that I looked as if I were dead. I was only 90 pounds and walking around with dry dusty looking skin. It hurt me to hear her say that but it helped me to become sick and tired of being under the influence. It was shortly after that, that I received my deliverance. God delivered me and I went from 90 pounds to 238 pounds.

I am always in church and I try to have a relationship with the leaders of churches which helps me to stay focused. It is when we lose focus that the enemy is there to get us whichever way he can.

October 2015, made sixteen years that I have been clean and I thank God for the people that have prayed for me. I can truly say that prayer changes things. I would not have made it this far without being active in church and leaning and depending on God.

The first step in finding my voice in my valley experience was to be honest with myself. I had to admit that I was messed up, that I was no longer submissive to God, I was not a good wife, I was a bad mother which caused my children to look at me funny and were ashamed at times to be around me at times. I had to admit that I needed to be reunited with God and that grace was going to run out and I would end up in hell if I did not straighten my life up.

It was at this point that I knew that I needed to love God and myself in order to love others as Christ loved me. Also, in reading and studying the word of God, I had to allow the Holy Scripture to shape and form Christ in me.

I encourage you not to get complacent in the valley, but seek God so that you will gravitate to the place where God wants to take you with minimum distractions.

Acknowledgement

Without Jesus Christ as My Lord and Savior, I would not have experienced the Joy of the Lord as my Strength. I thank you Lord for your patience towards me and imparting within me that I can do "all things through Christ that gives me strength.

I want to thank two of the most important individuals in my life that gave me purpose and strength to endure a challenging journey.

To my daughters, Lynee Layne Urban and Stephanie Marcella Layne: when you were both born, you became my priority, and my joy.

You truly are "Daddy's Girls" even as adult woman, and along with my granddaughters, Amani, Kayla, Eliana, and son in law Christopher, I am proud to be "Papa" - *Apostle Steven Layne.*

My Name is Steven and I Found My Voice

Steven Layne

My name is Steven Layne. I was born in November 1958, in Washington DC General Hospital. But I was raised on Long Island, NY as a child. I was the second oldest of three boys and two girls. The truth is - there were three fathers between the five of us.

It is interesting how you can grow up in the same household as your siblings and yet have different experiences. It wasn't long before I started noticing the difference between how my younger siblings were disciplined by "their father", versus how I was disciplined. The man who raised me exercised discipline that was so severe, I told people that the swollen lip and jaw came when I "fell off my bicycle." When you grow up feeling rejected; feeling like you just didn't "fit in", you learn to cope and so I created your own "world" in my room.

I always thought my older sister and I had the same father until I would hear how "her father" was killed in a cliff accident, but they never would say, "Both of your fathers were killed in a cliff accident." This is what added to me feeling different.

I had three career goals growing up, I was raised Catholic and wanted to become a priest, but when a Nun told me Priest could not marry, I scratched that plan right on the spot. Then I wanted to be an actor, but was told most would-be actors are waiters "hoping to be discovered". Ok, scratch that plan because I was not going to be a "waiter of tables". Therefore, that left me with Plan C. I was going to become a Police Officer, but that meant going to college; and after High School, I was sick of school. My Mom would not let me become a "freeloader", so I found a part time dish washing job that paid $2.20 an hour, and decided to enroll in the Community College.

From 1977-1980, I studied Criminal Justice at a Nassau Community College on Long Island, NY. I was fascinated with learning the law and court-case studies. I decided to travel as far as south as North Carolina to take Police Exams because my goal was to become a Police Officer somewhere by the age of 21. In 1980, there were three States I was considering for my career: Virginia, Maryland, and New York City Police Dept. I scored my highest grade for NYPD, but I did not think I was "tough enough" to be a New York City Cop. However, a neighbor who had family in law enforcement said to me, "Steven, just join for 3 years and you will learn enough to work anywhere in the country." Therefore, in January 26, 1981, 2 months after I turned 22 years old, I was sworn into the New York City Police Academy for 6 months of training. I finally completed my goal. I made it!

My name is Steven, and I am now a New York City Police Officer.

One morning in the summer of 1981, I had a "one-sided conversation" with a "voice" in my head. It was a Sunday morning, 8:50am. I opened my eyes from sleep and heard a voice say, "Go to Church". I got up and made it to the 10:00am Catholic Mass. That one-sided conversation was the beginning of a thought provoking question that I would later ask God. "God, I know if something happened to me, people would say nice things about me, but if something happened to me, what would you say about me? God, how am I supposed to live my life, according to you?"

This began a 2-3 month journey in which I would go to "Mass" 2-4 times a week in search of that answer. Then one day, while on foot patrol at "King's Park" in Jamaica Queens, NY, my path crossed with a young lady who "looked familiar", but I could quite place where I knew her. She recognized me right away, and called out my name, "Steven? Is that you? Congratulations on becoming a Police Officer. We went to the same High School and you graduated after my brother." I was pleasantly surprised. She had a very nice smile, 5'2 110 pounds, and shoulder length hair.

We met for lunch and as I was going to take my first bite, she asked, "Aren't you going to bless your food?" Oh, that's right; she's religious. I didn't think my standard prayer meant anything so I asked her to "say grace". I used this lunch date as my opportunity to ask about God and how I was supposed to live my life. I would pick her up from college and we would ride home together. She told me that the Bible says I must be "Born Again", but I always said when I do something, I want to be 100%. I did attend her church and couldn't understand why church was 3-4 hours on when at Mass, I was in by 10am, and out by 11am. Nonetheless, I liked hearing the "Bishop" in the 3-piece suit "Preach" what God's Word says in the Bible. I enjoyed the hand clapping, foot stomping choir that looked great in their robes. One another occasion a "Brother" in the Church talked to me about "getting saved", but my standard response worked for me.

Then that "one-sided" voice decided to have a private conversation with me when I was driving a patrol car. Out of nowhere, the "voice" asked me this:

Voice: "Steven, do you like baseball?

Me: "Yes, I like baseball".

Voice: "What happens when a batter gets two strikes against him?"

Me: "Well, one more strike and the batter is out."

Voice: "Steven, you have DENIED ME two times, ONE MORE time and you will never get the opportunity again!"

Stop the car! Whoa! OMG! I was shaking! I begged God not to let anything happen to me. I needed to get back to the 3-4 hour church service. But it was a Thursday and I needed God to protect me until Sunday evening. Please God! Please!

April 4, 1982 was a Sunday. I went to Mass in the morning and drove to the Bronx NY to that "Pentecostal/ Holiness Church". Ironically, my friend, "Kay" (not her real name), preached the evening message. To be truthful, I don't remember what the sermon was about, but then one of the brothers asked if anyone wanted prayer. Sitting on the back pew, I looked around and then raised my hand. After all, I wasn't going to turn down prayer. But then the brother told me to "come on down."

Geeze. I just wanted prayer; not to take "the longest walk" with everybody staring at me. But I knelt down and repeated the "Sinner's Prayer" and felt this wave hit me from my head to my toes and back up and down again. In an instant, I knew I was "Born Again". I knew that this Jesus that I heard about in the Catholic Church and now this Holiness Church was real. I wanted to cry, but "Oh No, I'm a cop", and I am not crying in front of these church people.

My name is Steven. I am now a Born Again Christian on April 4, 1982.

I did not know this, but Kay had actually planned on telling me she was not going to see me anymore because I was not "saved" and she had to "watch out for her soul." But God had other plans.

Kay and I continued seeing each other and then at 24 years old, on August 27, 1983, we married. I now had an opportunity to be "Godly husband". I was devoted to "Kay" and was in love with her. We did everything together. If you saw Kay, I was not too far away. She was still in college and after a year and an half being married, Kay dropped a bomb. "Steven, I don't love you completely. I only love you half way. I'm not sure I was supposed to marry you." I was confused. What am I not doing? I know God put us together? Maybe I'm not doing enough? I'll try harder. I'll read my bible more and ask the Holy Spirit to help me to love "Kay" as Jesus loves the Church. I would keep praying, "Lord show me what I'm doing wrong. I thought maybe if I did more, she would realize she had a good man given to her by God.

We were very dedicated to the Denomination, and in October 1986, I was appointed Pastor over a small church. Later that year I would hear it again. "Steven, I don't love you completely." But then we got news. Yes, you guessed it; Kay was pregnant with our first child. How could someone who "doesn't love me completely" explain getting pregnant and wanting to have a family? I knew our first born was special. You see, my birthday is November 21, 1958. My first born was born November 12, 1985. See if you can figure it out. When "my oldest" was birthed, I screamed, "She looks like me!" Not only was I the happiest man alive, I loved Kay even more as a woman for sacrificing herself for those 9 months.

On October 5, 1988, my "youngest" daughter was born. Because this pregnancy was completely opposite from the first. I told "Kay" that we would be a family of four. No more children. I did not want her to experience another challenging pregnancy. Our family was set.

I thought some things would change with being a family; being Pastor and Kay as the Co-Pastor. But the truth is from 1985 -2004, sometimes twice a year I heard those words, "I don't love you. I wasn't supposed to marry you; I was only supposed to win you to the Lord. I feel that God is punishing me for marrying you." The words started to wear me down mentally. I began to tell myself, "Steven, you're just not good enough.

In 1996, one year after we purchased the home, Kay told me she was "disconnected" for years from the marriage. However, I held out for hope. I fasted for 9 months asking God to "fix" me. I was starting a new Ministry, I still had to be there for the members; I still had to preach and teach. I still took my girls to their practices and showed up for every softball game; be in the stands while my younger daughter was on the cheerleader squad, not to mention band practice and concerts and going on family vacations together. And yet, I started to feel lonely.

Kay doesn't know to this day that I found out she told another male about some personal things I was experiencing with my health. A woman should never compare her companion to a man who may have more going for himself than their spouse. I would tell myself, "If you had a degree, and made more money, and had a "big Church", and drove a luxury car and was popular in the ministry like the other well-known Ministers were, she would love me."

Sleepless nights made it dangerous as a Police Officer because I needed to be alert, and there were times I dozed off right in my car at a traffic light. I know it is said that you shouldn't stay married for the sake of children, but because I did not know my father, I refused to do that to my girls.

I made it to the 20-year mark and it was time to retire from the police force. I appreciated the retirement party she gave me. One year after I retired, Kay said she wanted a divorce. She was going to give me custody of the girls, but then changed her mind. My oldest daughter was now away in college and my youngest has one more year in high school. It is now hard to Pastor; I was just existing and going through Pastoral motions. I am beginning to feel like a failure as a man and a Pastor, and now I'm convinced I'll never be good enough for any woman.

As I was in my computer room preparing a Bible study lesson, I suddenly felt a twitch on the right side of my face. It felt as if my right eye was closing. As I got up to look in the mirror at my face, I heard the Lord say, "Steven that is from stress; next is a stroke. And if you have a stroke, you will not be good to yourself, to me, nor your girls." So I asked the Lord to release me from this marriage and He replied, "Steven, I released you a long time ago! There are some things going on that you don't know about."

With my face twitching, I went down stairs to have a conversation. I wanted to know what I could do in the future to fix me. I wanted to know how I can improve myself as a husband; as a man, because in spite of the dissolving of this marriage, I still love marriage. So this was the conversation:

Me: "Kay, I will give you the divorce, but you will have to file it and have me served. But let me ask you this, "Why is it that you don't want to be married to me anymore?"

Kay: "Steven, I do not love you and I never did love you."

At that moment, I did not know who she was anymore. I felt like the home was no longer mine. My daughters was not present to see the exchange, but in that moment, I felt like everything (except my daughters) was a lie. What was real about this marriage?

In two days, she handed me the business card of the divorce attorney. The papers were filed in February 2004, On May 11, 2004, the divorce was finalized. I moved from a four bedroom house to a basement apartment. No working stove; no heat; basement windows with very little natural light.

I stepped down from Pastoring after 17 years as Senior Pastor/Apostle and founder; I was depressed. I felt like a failure. And the twitching to the right side continued.

Hi, my name is Steven, and I felt like I am a dead man walking.

And then something happened. I think I was watching a television program and a therapist said these words; "The best thing that a divorce parent can show their children is that they have moved on, are well-adjusted". Suddenly inner peace was returning to my life." Hallelujah! I asked God if I could move somewhere to start my life over. I nicknamed myself, "Starting over Steve". The hard part was telling my daughters however. I packed my Honda Accord with my 32 inch color TV and sent all my clothes via the brown truck service to my mom's house. I moved to South Carolina, got a job as a substitute teacher and found a place to stay.

Hi. My Name is Steven, and I was starting to regroup.

It would be around 3 years later that I tried my hands at marriage a second time but it was a disaster and lasted less than 6 months. I still was 'damaged goods.
The turnaround came when I had another conversation with the Lord.

Me: "Lord, how can you use me when I failed as a Pastor, a husband both times?"

God: "Steven, didn't you know before I created the foundation of the world that I knew you were going to be divorced twice, and lose your home and have bad credit? I never withdrew the Pastoral/Apostolic call from your life, because my gifts and callings are without repentance! "

I cried!

Me: "God. Who was I supposed to be when I was in my mother's womb? What was your original blueprint for my life?"

"Steven, I will show you layer by layer over time."

I would become an Assistant Pastor in 2008 before stepping down in May 2015 to assist in another smaller Ministry and covenant with a Global Intercessory Prayer Ministry. I have discovered and rediscovered the "authentic" Steven that the Father, Son, and Holy Spirit always purposed me to be. The restoration process continues and I love the person that I am and can't wait to cover the one that the Lord has in marriage for me. I'm going to let the Lord put me in the right place at the right time. I just sense that I will know it when I meet my "bone of bone and flesh of flesh". There is so much more that this journey has taught me. Stay tune for the rest. In the meantime, I have started over still loving "My Girls" and now my three grands. As far as my former wives are concerned, I wish only the best for them.

My name is Steven and I have finally found my Voice.

JOYCE SAMUELS

"Whoever dwells in the shelter of the Most High will rest in the shadow of the Almighty. ² I will say of the LORD, "He is my refuge and my fortress, my God, in whom I trust." Psalm 91:1-2

Elder Joyce Samuels is a devoted and dynamic woman of God who strives to encourage, equip, and empower others through the wisdom of Jesus Christ and the power of prayer. She has overcome many childhood obstacles, disappointments and trials that led her to be an advocate for children, an educator, and motivator by enhancing the intellectual and spiritual capacity of others.

Elder Samuels has demonstrated her commitment to education naturally and spiritually, with a degree in

Education and a medical certification. She was the proprietress of a childcare center and pre-school for 22 years and a principal for 4 years. Elder Samuels is a licensed and ordained elder with certifications in leadership, mentorship and prophetic gifting.

Elder Samuels is energized and excited by the endless opportunities to spread the gospel and share God's love. Her greatest joy is to help people in need. She believes that we are most like Christ when we are in service. She has a heart for all people and operates in God's wisdom to cultivate a love of self, community and service in children, women and men. She aligns herself with the voice of God, to serve and meet the needs of people, spiritually and emotionally.

Elder Samuels has a desire to reach all souls, regardless or ethnicity, gender or generation and is an exemplification of a miracle and survivor. As the literary lead and co-author of the inspirational book, *"Rescued for His Glory: Stories of Hope, Triumph and Wholeness"*, she brought together 16 women from across the nation to share their testimonies, in an attempt to have transparent dialogue about the life issues we encounter but suffer silently through. It was a groundbreaking and successful endeavor that created solid spiritual relationships among the women who participated and many of the men and women who read and could see themselves in the shared testimonies.

Elder Samuels is a loving and devoted wife and mother to her husband, Keith D. Samuels, Sr. and her five (5) children. She is widely known for her powerful prayer life and the gift of faith which fuels her desire to continue learning and growing in Christ so she can continue to teach the truth of the Gospel for the sole purpose of winning souls to the Kingdom.

KIM A. DISTEFANO

Born in Barbados, West Indies, **Pastor Kim A. DiStefano** is an accomplished and results oriented consultant and master facilitator with over 15 years of experience working with individuals, teams, and executives, creating vision and structure where there is none and developing end-to-end human resources solutions.

Kim is currently President and CEO of Oracle HR Consulting Group, a full range of human resource management consulting firm. She has been a valued advisor and business partner across a broad range of industries. The depth and breadth of her knowledge in organizational behavior and leadership development has made her a sought after keynote speaker for conferences and positions her as a thought leader on various leadership and diversity/inclusion panels.

With a heart for people and a passion for women's empowerment and youth development, Kim was raised up and trained as a Pastor at Kingdom Nation Ministries under the leadership of Apostle Kevin Whitson. Her passion and love for God comes from truly being born again and her conviction that only God can transform people and their lives to enable them to realize and reach their God-given purpose. Undoubtedly, her anointing is to assist with establishing ministry and ministering to women while also nurturing and developing the next generation to walk according to the Word and will of God. She believes that we are most like Christ when we are in service to others.

Kim founded, "The Deborah Movement", a non-profit organization which focuses on interactive, creative programs and workshops designed to equip, empower and encourage women to achieve success personally and professionally. Her ministry experiences have been diverse and dynamic. She is committed to learning and growing in Christ so she can better reach people of all backgrounds and serve as a role model. As a child of God and a teacher of the gospel, her contributions to ministry and to the community have been innumerable, invaluable, and definitely kingdom-building.

Kim is a co-author of *"Rescued for His Glory: Stories of Hope, Triumph and Wholeness"*. She is married to Christopher Pitts and together they parent five children, Montez (24), Shannon (21), Marquis (21), Makala (18) and Nathaniel (13). When she's not running her company, being a mother and involved in ministry, Kim is an avid reader, loves extreme sports and watching The First 48.

SERRICA JACKSON

Serrica Jackson is a loving mother of two young boys 10 and 3 years old. She is happily married and a loving wife of 3 years. She and her beautiful family currently resides in the Maryland but originated from Atlanta Georgia.

Mrs. Jackson is currently enrolled in college studying for her Bachelor's Degree in Psychology and is pursuing to become a Social Worker.

She enjoys spending quality time with her family, reading and writing. Her goal is to complete her own story and finish her book.

EVELYN M. JACKSON

Evelyn M. Jackson is a happily married wife of 17 years to the absolute love of her life, Sylvester D. Jackson. She is a mother of two very handsome sons, Sylvester IV (19) and David (10) and currently resides in Bowie, MD. Mrs. Jackson is the CEO of The Jackson Transportation Company, a family owned and operated business. She holds a certification in Youth Trauma and is a well-known Team Mom for the Bowie Broncos and is committed and very active in her son's activities. She is also currently the Woodmore Elementary PTA Treasurer, as well as a volunteer in her son's school.

Evelyn is a wonderful, dedicated neighbor especially to the Seniors and a Loving community Family Daycare provider. The Jackson family attends Reid Temple church in Glendale, Maryland.

Mrs. Jackson is a true Friend to many, but known to be a stranger to none. Her outgoing personality and beautiful smile compliments her dynamic genuine character.

VALERIE JOHNSON-PHILSON

Valerie Johnson-Philson. was born to Minister Barbara Johnson-Mack and Edward Johnson, January 6, 1966. She have one sister who is 18 months younger than me. She have been married to Craig Philson, since August 3, 1986. They have four children, Craig, Lucretia, Edward and Daniel and six grandchildren Remia, Saiya, Jaylen, Destiny, D'Marco, and Ja'Liyah.

She has worked for Housing and Urban Development for 14 years. She am co-author of a book, "Rescued for His Glory." She began her Christian college education at Washington Bible College in June 2010. She later graduated from Lancaster Bible College in August 2014, with a BA in Business Administration. She is currently attending Capital Seminary, pursuing a Master's degree in Leadership.

She is currently serving as a Minister in training at Praise Redemption Worship Center, under the leadership of Bishop Nathaniel Huggins.

STEVEN LAYNE

Steven Layne, was born in 1958 in Washington DC to the late Earthalee M. (Laboard) Layne of Johns Island, South Carolina and is the second oldest of 5 brothers and sisters. His family moved from Washington DC to Long Island, New York, where he attended grade school, and as a Catholic, he also attended 3 years of Catholic School where Steven expressed interest in becoming a Catholic Priest.

Because he was told Catholic Priest were forbidden to marry, Steven abandoned the idea, and upon graduating high School, attended Nassau Community College where he studied Criminal Justice and pursued a career in Law Enforcement.

In January 1981, Steven was accepted into the New York City Police Academy, and upon completion of the academy was sworn in as a New York City Police Officer. During his career, Steven Layne worked in narcotics as an undercover officer, street patrol, Highway Patrol, and finished his career teaching in an Anti-Gang, Drug, and Gun violence Unit. Apostle Layne was also the Vice President of "Police Officers for Christ", formally known as "Cops for Christ" in the New York City Police Dept.

It was during his early years as a police officer that Steven desired to know how God wanted him to live his life, after having the Gospel shared with him, on April 4th, 1982, Steven accepted Jesus Christ into his life, and joined a Pentecostal/ Holiness Church called The Church of God of Prophecy. 4 years later, in 1986, Steven was appointed Pastor in the Church of God of Prophecy for 10 years. Apostle Layne was also the Vice President of "Police Officers for Christ", formally known as "Cops for Christ" in the New York City Police Dept.

In 1995, Pastor Layne founded and pastored another Ministry called Reach Out & Touch Ministries Int'l.Inc. and was called, ordained and confirmed to the Office of Apostle in October 1995. Reach Out and Touch Ministries Int'l, Inc. is still ministering today in Staten Island, New York.

In February 2001, after 20 years in the Police Dept. Steven retired and relocated to South Carolina in August 2004, where he started attending Church House of Ministries Christian Church Worldwide, located in Ladson, SC. In 2008, Steven was ordained the Assistant Pastor where He served faithfully until June 2015.

Because the Lord has never withdrawn the Office of the Apostle's call on Apostle Layne's life, the Lord has released him from The Church House of Ministries and has planted the Facebook Ministry of Reach Out & Touch Ministries Int'l, Inc. NY/SC via the social media. Early this year 2015, Apostle Layne has been introduced to KRGA under the mentorship/ covering of Apostle Ron Toliver and GIPA under the covering of Prophetess and Executive Overseer Darlene Hunter Fant.

Apostle Layne is mandated to the call to the Kingdom of God and to intercede for Gods men and women.

Apostle Steven Layne is a proud father of 2 daughters who live in Chicago and New York and grandfather of 3 grand-daughters.

Finally, "Apostle Steven" wants you to know he does not apologize for being a sports fan of the NY Jets, Notre Dame & NY Yankees

www.ingramcontent.com/pod-product-compliance
Lightning Source LLC
Chambersburg PA
CBHW070459090426
42735CB00012B/2625